HOUSES NOW
ZEN INTERIORS

Edition 2007

Author: Carles Broto
Graphic designer & production: Oriol Vallès
Text: contributed by the architects, edited William George
and Marta Rojals

© Carles Broto i Comerma
Jonqueres, 10, 1-5
08003 Barcelona, Spain
Tel.: +34 93 301 21 99
Fax: +34-93-301 00 21
E-mail: info@linksbooks.net
www. linksbooks.net

HOUSES NOW
ZEN INTERIORS

index

INTRODUCTION

Zen Interiors responds to the modern inner urge to pare down and slow down felt by many. These are serene, uncluttered havens from the outside world, achieved through the harmonious application of concepts central to Zen: simplicity, inner calm, harmony. Transferred to the sanctuary of the home, we find: simplicity of layout, subtlety of light, calming tones and clean lines in architecture is a working method in which the aesthetic seeks all its force and capacity to astonish in a simple way and without superfluous elements. It is said that "less is more", and the spaces are adapted to an idea of life that is intended to be simple, allowing the fascination to be shown in the linearity of a wall, in the smooth textures of a floor, in a reserved space, in the hole as a structuring element of this architecture that seeks its essences. Absence is therefore a virtue that exalts formality, imagination and an appetite for creating new sensations with the minimum intervention. It is the architecture of silence, of subtle expressions that seek the complicity of its occupants and of the context in which it is located. The simple design of buildings or public spaces, far more than a reduction to simplicity. It also requires a great effort -often even greater than that made by other architectural tendencies -because fewer elements means fewer possibilities and alternatives, and it is more difficult to achieve amenable, illuminated rooms that have a welcoming and relaxing atmosphere. The dialogue between the buildings and the public takes place both in the forms and in spirituality: it is the architecture of calm, reflection and meditation.

Marco Savorelli

Nicola's Home

Milan, Italy

Photographs: Matteo Piazza

On the concept evolution of the recuperation possibilities of an old roof attic is founded the bet between the client and designers: to start from zero, working in abstract on "home system" functions and utilities, beginning from recuperation of an unitarian, primary, elementary space, translating old function into new, mitigated and simplified forms.

Discrete presence, operative spaces like bathroom, kitchen and wardrobe translate themselves into monolithic volumes that, reduced into simple forms, gain plastically authority creating new ways, background, bonds and articulations of the perceptive space system.

This is project where the historical memory of the site meets a rigorous formal research. A well balanced experimentation with new spaces preserving the existing quality of light. The result is a playful alternation of volumes and moods, a fluid exchange between the existing and the designed space. These are characteristics of a project which evolved from the intense dialogue between the architect and the client, aiming to achieve a minimalist aesthetics and at the same time volumetric and functional complexity. This is not a mere operation of interior decoration but the creation of volumes to be lived in and "live with" in a completely modern and innovative way. The space acquires both a jocose and a reflexive quality.

When entering this apartment the visual impact is instantaneous —a nearly flash-like perception of the space— which reveals the equilibrium between matter and light. The natural daylight traces delicate designs on the neat surfaces, shadows in perpetual movement creating a simple and primordial game of light and darkness.

Light was treated as an element of the construction whose function consists not only in lighting the dwelling but also in defining spaces inside it. In this sense, the strategic arrangement of top lighting gives the environment a very peculiar vertical dimension.

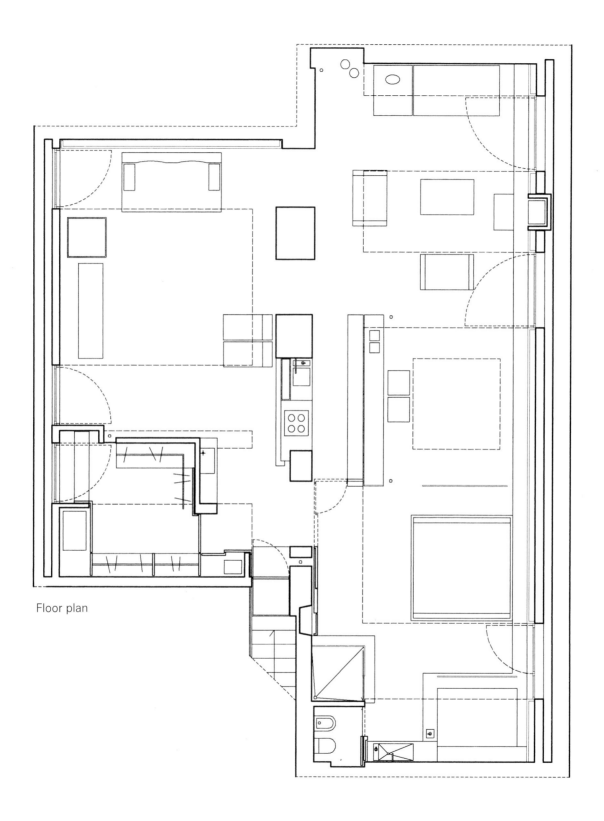

Floor plan

Bonetti Kozerski Studio

DK Apartment

New York, USA

Photographs: Matteo Piazza

The project features a master bedroom suite that includes a dressing room and bathroom gallery; a large living room and dining room that is connected to the terraces with a stone platform that runs throughout; a meditation room and "spa" bathroom, a chef's kitchen and preparation kitchen/pantry, a house manager's office and a maid's suite. The house is furnished with custom furniture designed by Bonetti/Kozerski Studio, Asian antique pieces and some contemporary pieces. Floors in the public spaces feature cross cut travertine in 1.2 meter square tiles, while the bathrooms use larger pieces of travertine on the walls and floors. Flooring in the master suite is a tatami style wool sisal, in a color matching the stone. The walls are highly polished Venetian stucco in an ivory color. The ceilings are custom colored ivory paint. The kitchen features a combination of natural teak, stainless steel lower cabinets, frosted glass upper cabinets and a basalt volcanic stone counter top.

The project involved the combining of two large apartments at the top of a 1929 building on Central Park West. Even before starting the design we concentrated our efforts on finding a way to have the client's full understanding of the spatial concept in order to win her trust in something that was going to be quite different from the traditional New York upscale apartment. We built a full-scale model of the design after demolishing all the non-structural walls of the apartment. We employed a theatrical company that built fabric walls held in place by spring-poles. Reading a plan or fully understanding a model can be complicated for a client: building a full scale model permitted the client to literally walk into the design, comprehend it and familiarize himself with it before committing to the expense. The fabric walls could be instantly moved, giving the opportunity to verify a spatial solution, change it or incorporate the client's suggestions. Once satisfied with the layout and the furniture, which was also mocked up full size, we did a survey and transferred the final design on paper. Some of the architectural solutions derived directly from techniques employed in the full size model. The lighting was designed by Arnold Chan from London's Isometrix, who collaborated with us before on the Donna Karan Store on Madison Avenue.

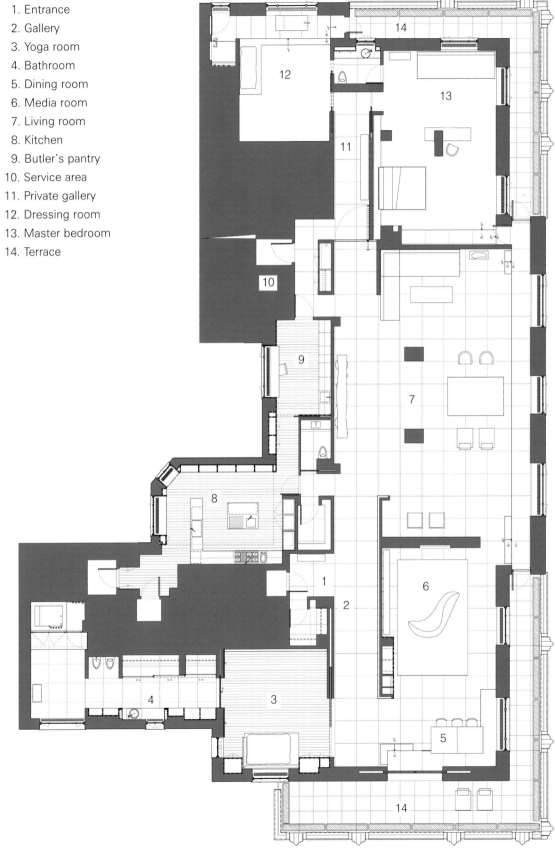

1. Entrance
2. Gallery
3. Yoga room
4. Bathroom
5. Dining room
6. Media room
7. Living room
8. Kitchen
9. Butler's pantry
10. Service area
11. Private gallery
12. Dressing room
13. Master bedroom
14. Terrace

Floors in the public spaces feature cross cut travertine in 1.2 meter square tiles, while the walls are highly polished Venetian stucco in an ivory color.

SCDA Architects

Teng Residence

Singapore, Singapore

Photographs: Peter Mealin

This house, designed for a single male professional and his mother, is located on a tight suburban lot where plot ratios have been intensified and the height increased to three floors. One atypical feature of this home is the inclusion of a prayer/meditation room.

The suburbs of Singapore have been highly urbanized as the result of changes in zoning regulations. In the case of this project, the neighboring house is less than four meters away, making privacy a key concern.

The house is conceived as a latticed, two-story wooden box, constructed entirely of steel and wood and suspended above ground level.

A sheer wall (meant to form a visual barrier) has been built one meter from the building on the side facing a neighboring house. This one-meter slot allows light to wash against the sheer wall, reflecting it back toward the house.

All the plumbing and services are organized in a zone to the right of the party wall. A granite internal reflecting pool is located under the central, trellised skylight; while a slender steel and timber bridge connects the two halves of the program.

The facades are designed with a double skin. Fixed timber louvers are angled down to allow views of the exterior, while ensuring privacy from street level. The facade's glazing has openable panels allowing for natural ventilation.

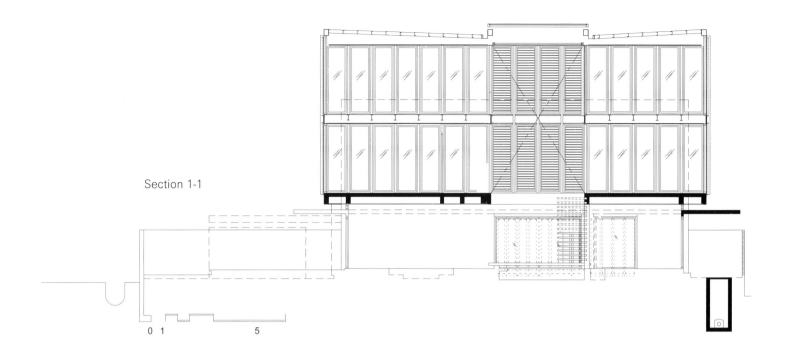

Section 1-1

0 1   5

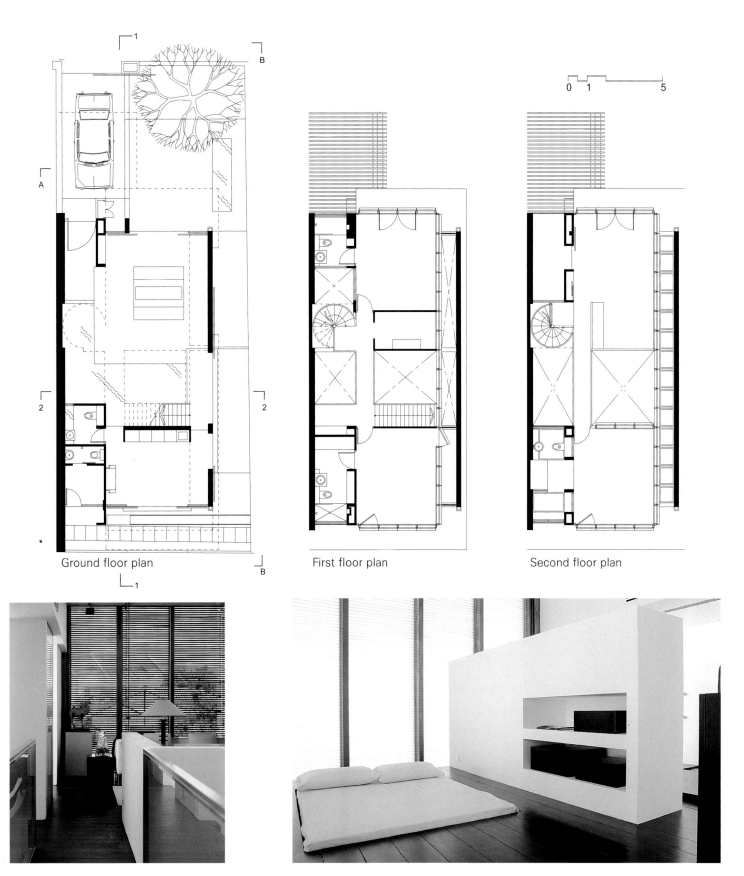

Ground floor plan

First floor plan

Second floor plan

0 1   5

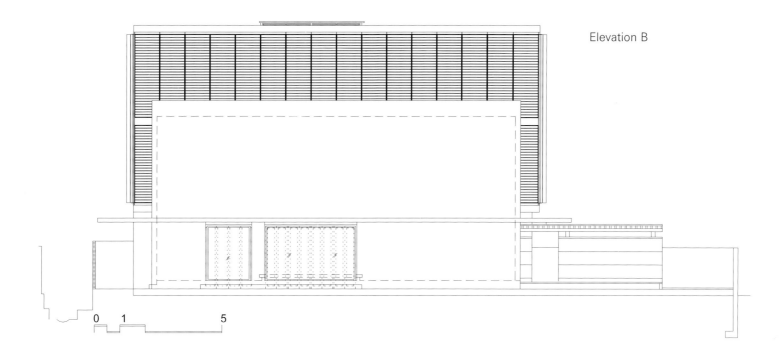

Elevation B

0 1   5

Only at ground level are the windows visually unobstructed to allow views of the narrow garden between the two houses. The living room is well-supplied with natural light from above (the central well) and the side. Light is increased by white walls and floor.

Elevation A

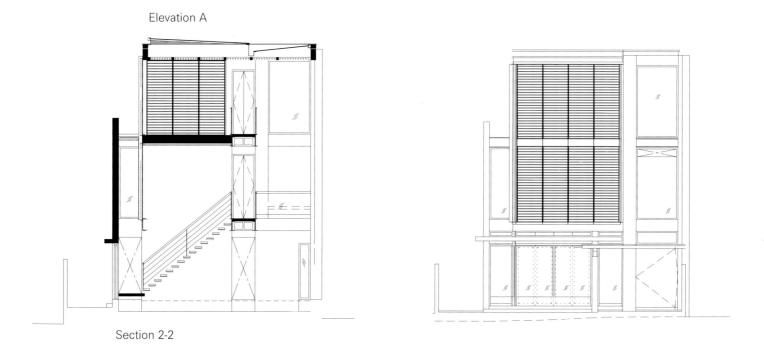

Section 2-2

Vincent van Duysen

Town Houses in Flanders

Flanders, Belgium

Photographs: Jan Verlinde

The project consists of the refurbishment of a classic 1930's row house with a fairly restricted width and a deep plan.

The house is situated between five similar row houses by the same architect and from the same period; which is why the front elevation has only been restored instead of entirely redone.

The deep plan of the existing house made it very dark, so Van Duysen has instead opted for an open plan with a glazed central void over three stories, visually connecting all the spaces vertically and horizontally, with daylight pouring through a large rooflight and a completely glazed back elevation.

The impressive spatial qualities are emphasized by several factors. From one side, the unrestricted views from the front toward the back of the house on all levels (entering through the front door one can see the garden gate in the back garden). Views are also provided by two voids on the rooflight and the central lightwell; the completely glazed back elevation gives views of the old industrial buildings and chimneys.

The materials used in the building process consist of flush planes of dark tinted oak against a background of white plastered walls and have been carefully proportioned to emphasize the spatial system of the house. Large planes of glass divide the structure and organization of the plan.

The whole building is opened toward the garden through the completely glazed elevation, whereby the window frames again reflect the structure inside. At the same time, the walled garden elongates the space of the dining and cooking area and, combined with the void above the dining room and the use of identical stone flooring both outside and in, effectively pulls the internal and external space together into one unified whole. The patio wall marks the end of the external dining area and creates a kind of "garden room", with a framed view of the garden.

Vincent van Duysen

Finca in Mallorca

Mallorca, Spain

Photographs: Alberto Piovano

This house maintains the characteristics and spirit of the original Majorcan vernacular architecture on the outside, while creating a contemporary image on the inside.

The project began with an old country house in the inland part of the island with a theatrical portico of the main facade and two adjacent buildings that function as the custodian's lodging and the owner's office. Van Duysen also worked on the design of the garden, creating visual connections by means of paving in a particular composite of concrete and local stone, also used for the flooring of the buildings to create a sense of indoor-outdoor continuity. An imposing wooden enclosure defines a true barrier, both physical and visual, between the private residential space and the custodian's lodging, or between the interior and exterior worlds.

As visitors cross the threshold they have the impression of entering a large patio, which is nevertheless intimate and welcoming.

The only theatrical presence in this space is a washstand made of a single block of stone, inserted in a niche. This sensation continues inside the main house. The entrance area is an empty room, with wood paneling on the walls, concealing the access to the guest bathroom. From the entrance one proceeds to the large kitchen/dining room or to the staircase leading to the upper level housing the bedrooms.

The rigor of the furnishing solutions for each room, based on simple planes and elementary volumes, solids and space, elements for storage and display, seems to make reference to a monastic model of living. The sensory richness of the materials used (sanded and stained oak, stone, marble, ceramics) gives these solutions an air of extreme elegance. Meticulous attention was paid to detail and to the choice of delicate color combinations to create a relaxing atmosphere for this holiday home.

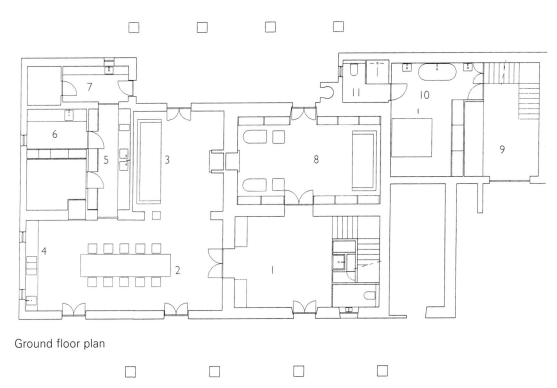

Ground floor plan

1. Main entrance
2. Dining room
3. Living room
4. Kitchen
5. Scullery
6. Laundry
7. Back entrance
8. Library
9. Guesthouse entrance
10. Guesthouse bedroom
    & bathroom
11. Guesthouse shower
12. Guesthouse kitchen
13. Guesthouse terrace
14. Nighthall
15. Master bedroom
16. Dressing master
    bedroom
17. Master bathroom
18. Child's bedroom
19. Child's bathroom
20. Mainhouse terrace

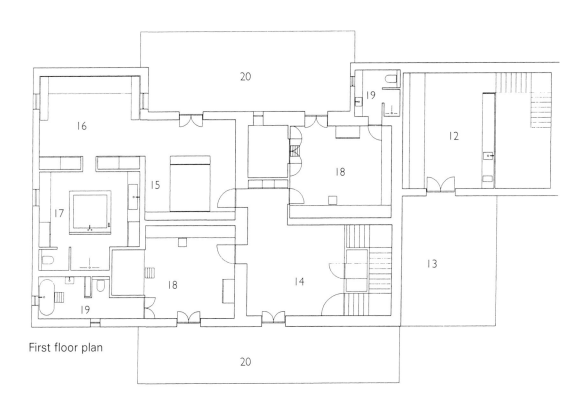

First floor plan

The architecture of Vicent van Duysen is based on premises such as simplicity and comfort, with a predominance of pure lines and an unadorned architecture. He thus builds exquisite spaces in which the light and the soft colors play a major role.

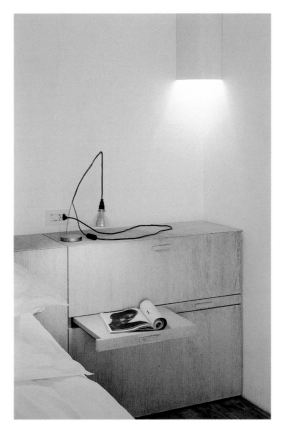

The washbasin located in the entrance area is housed in a natural wooden closet located at the bottom of the staircase leading to the upper floor.

Johnson Chou

Yolles Residence

Toronto, Canada

Photographs: Volker Seding

When Eric Yolles (son of renowned Canadian structural engineer Morden Yolles) wrote a program detailing every aspect of his new loft to be considered, he concluded with two words: "think penitentiary". The intention was not to create a space that would be harsh and cold, but one of calm and repose. He wanted a contemplative space with a minimum of spatial distraction, one with particular attention to materials and detail - that his loft would not contain any overt decorative embellishments or gratuitous design flourishes.

Housed in a converted warehouse in downtown Toronto, the 2,000SF loft is organized in a conventional strip with industrial windows at one end. All non-structural walls were removed and a wall dividing the public and private areas was replaced with a 30' sandblasted glass screen. Layering with sliding partitions, views through rooms change as these panels move and entice with sections of clear glass - transforming and revealing one area as they conceal another. The largest of these partitions - a dramatic section of 16' stainless steel - separates the bedroom from the living room. Inspired by the "Panopticon", a prison type that allows the warden to view all inmates from a single position, the design amplifies the voyeuristic pleasures of surveillance: a 10-inch strip of clear glass through which one can view the living areas from the sunken slate bathtub - true bachelor-pad indulgence, complete with built-in candleholders. Experimenting with the act of view-

ing, the bathing area is like a stage set where one enacts the self-conscious performance of both watching and being watched.

Designing everything essential to living directly into the space is an integral part of the designer's creative philosophy; creating 'a narrative of habitation' - or building a 'script' for the client. The bed (aluminum-clad and king-sized) is cantilevered from the wall so it appears to hover in mid-air. A glowing bedside 'command module' constructed of sandblasted glass slides open to access light switches, thermostat and telephone. Aluminum floor to ceiling storage closets span the entire length of the bedroom, holding and hiding all of the client's belongings.

Though bare and elemental, the liberal use of glass, aluminum, stainless steel and concrete impart a particular glow and warmth to the interior, specific to the materials themselves. Subtle nuances and reflections in the slate and metal reveal themselves through lighting, playing off surfaces, lending a sculptural, ephemeral quality to the bed and freestanding vanity. Using light as a theatrical element, halogen and fluorescent fixtures are used in a variety of combinations to re-define space, use, and mood. Intersecting ceiling-mounted recessed fluorescent lighting provides ambient lighting while halogen and accent lighting are strategically positioned to subtly highlight existing and new architectural details and textures.

1. Foyer

2. Powder room

3. Guest bedroom

4. Kitchen

5. Living room

6. Laundry

7. Bedroom

8. Storage

9. Vanity

10. Bath

11. Toilet

12. Shower

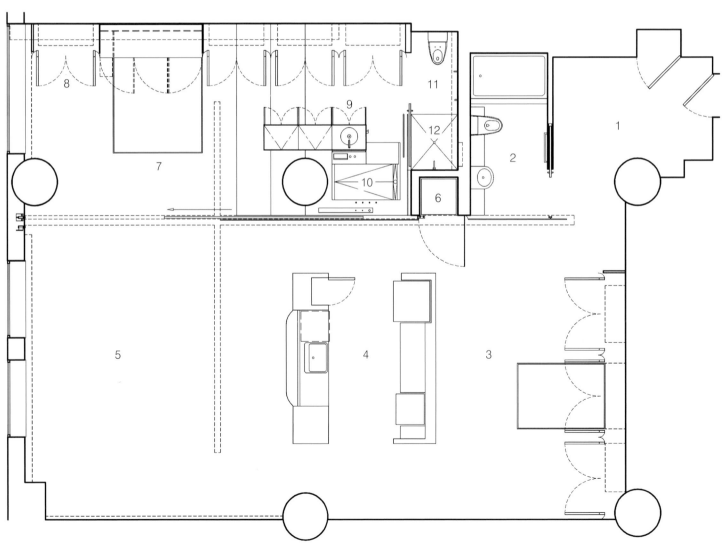

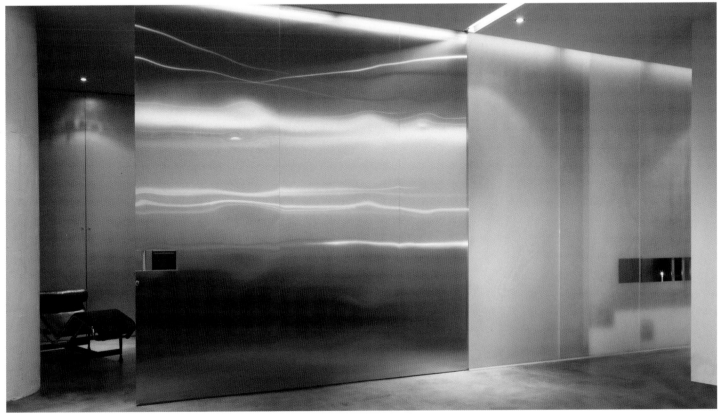

Though bare and elemental, the liberal use of glass, aluminum, stainless steel and concrete impart a particular glow and warmth to the interior, specific to the materials themselves.

Johnson Chou

Womb: work, office, meditation, base

Toronto, Canada

Photographs: Volker Seding

'Retreat' invokes more than escape – we retreat to contemplate, reflect and create, to harness the creativity and focus we sometimes lack. It is where we physically and intellectually rejuvenate, a place where books are written, design concepts formed - where one is creatively inspired.

A multi-functional (home/office) space, Womb (for work, office, meditation, base), recognizes that our refuge must fulfill a variety of needs. Designed to be four rooms in one, the space transforms as desired, maintaining an elementally ethereal aesthetic.

With furniture and cabinetry that pivot and disappear into walls and floors with a touch of a button, Womb offers four programmatic rooms that occupy the entire 600sqft (56 sqm) space; kitchen/dining, work/office, bedroom/living, spa/bath, all within a spare, Zen-like meditative environment. Womb proposes a 21st century 'machine for living' – concealing what isn't immediately necessary, eliminating visual distractions and quadrupling its spatial effectiveness.

The kitchen unit slides into the wall when not needed, and the empty space allows a table to pivot around, a clean work area with an unobstructed view across the pool to the exterior. Sink and work surfaces are hidden under covers that open to an upright position. In the center of the room, the bathing/reflecting pool and suspended stainless steel fireplace anchor the space as the only fixed elements. Expanding and contracting as needed, the washroom is situated centrally near the pool and fireplace. A "u"-shaped wall that conceals the bathroom slides to allow one to enter, or to enclose the occupant for privacy. When not in use, the wall automatically closes, completely regaining the space. The living area, separated by the pool from the work/kitchen space, contains a bed that disappears into the floor when not required, allowing a cantilevered couch to fold out from the wall.

The walls are a blank canvas for lighting to transform, fluorescents creating a cool white daytime space that recessed halogen lights turn to a warmer intimacy by evening. Further modulation is achieved with fiber-optics that "paint" the walls with variable hues.

1. Foyer
2. Pivoting table
3. Retractable kitchen
4. Bathroom
5. Whirlpool/bath
6. Bedroom
7. Fireplace

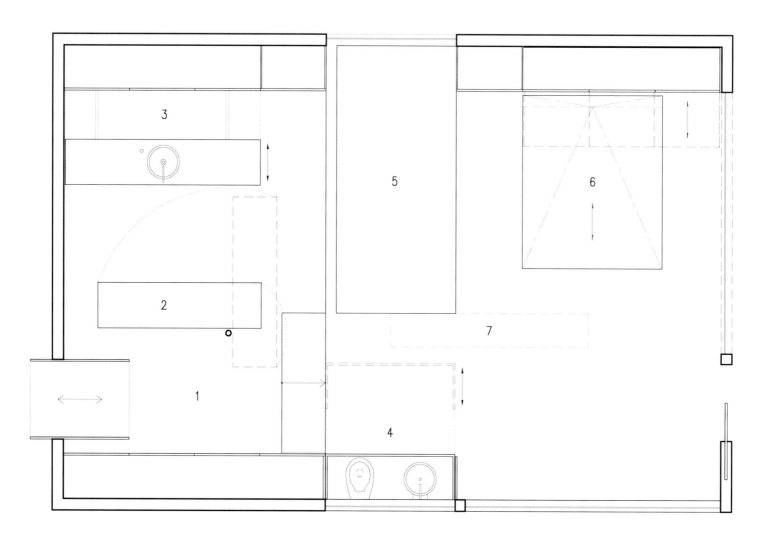

Animated by the ballet movements of the architectural elements, bathed in nuances of light, this is an environment designed to inspire reflection, creation and contemplation yet able to transform itself for living purposes. Womb is truly a base for work, office and meditation.

Shigeru Ban

Naked House

Kawagoe, Japan

Photographs: Hiroyuki Hirai

An unusual client commission requested a home that would "provide the minimum amount of intimacy, so that the members of the family are not isolated from each other - a home that would give each one the freedom to carry out individual activities in a shared atmosphere within the bosom of a close-knit family". The result is a roomy double-height space with uninterrupted sight lines from end to end. Instead of dividing walls demarcating individual bedrooms, the "private" spaces are open volumes equipped with wheels to give them mobility within this hangar-like space. The interior layout can be changed every day if desired; larger "rooms" can be instantly created by removing and stacking their sliding doors. Being lightweight, these volumes can also be wheeled outside in order to make full use of the available space. They can also be used as "bunks", with plenty of sturdy flat space above where kids can play or where objects can be stowed.

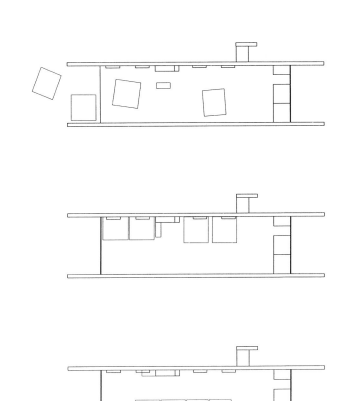

Layout variations

69

Eline Strijkers

Unit 9

Amsterdam, The Netherlands

Photographs: Teo Krijgsman

The floor plan nearly always provides the basis for the organization of functions; when a dwelling is organized vertically, using a multistory elevation as the point of departure, the result can have a completely different character. In this particular dwelling-cum-workplace the functions are connected to the walls and not to the floors.

This is how the existing shell of a harbor building (measuring some 2691 sq ft or 250 sqm) in Amsterdam-North has been approached. All supporting functions are enclosed volumes. Because work, storage, seating, eating, cooking, and sleeping are all components of a particular volume or surface, the space is almost entirely free of freestanding pieces of furniture.

The volumes unfold like independent sculptures, while at the same time making a free division of the space possible. Here, also, a vertical organization of the space is emphasized. There is a clear division between the ground floor and the other levels, which have been handled as a spatial whole.

The radical nature of the spatial concept lies mainly in the way that Strijkers has developed the unexpected materialization of her design, down to the smallest detail. At ground level, a different material was used to create transitions from one room to another. The materials used upstairs give terms like 'domesticity' and ' coziness' an entirely new frame of reference. Despite all the attention paid to space, form, materials and details, the rooms are not ruined by a profusion of design. The prevailing casual atmosphere is the result of an unpolished use of materials, a sense of openness between the various parts of this home/workspace and, in particular, the tendency toward collective use.

Ground floor plan

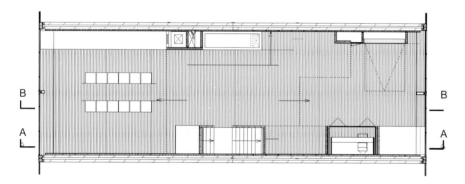

First floor plan

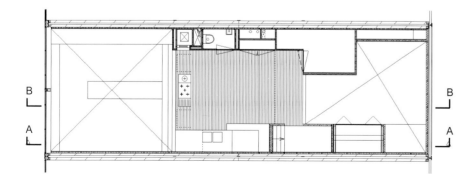

Second floor plan

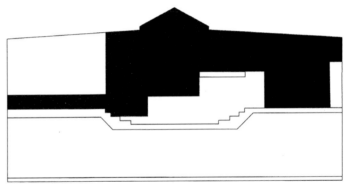

Concept drawing connected program

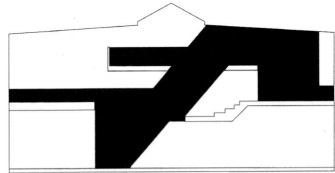

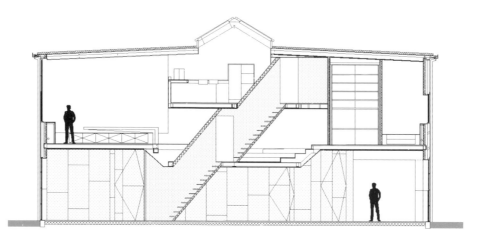

Section AA

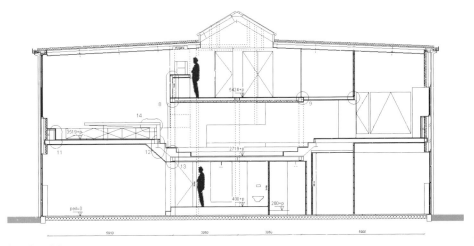

Section BB

Anouska Hempel

The Hempel

London, UK

Photographs: Kim Zwarts

Discreetly hidden just north of Hyde Park, the Hempel Hotel and Hempel Garden Square are a unique phenomenon in London.

The simplicity and silence of the Orient and their metamorphism into the Western world, with the most innovative global technology, create a very special hotel. A row of perfectly restored white Georgian houses and a private garden surrounded by trees give little hint of the remarkable transformation within.

Crossing the main entrance is almost a mystical experience. Beyond it, the visitor finds a wide empty space, in which the only outstanding element is the monolithic block of the reception desk, which recalls the calm and contemplative atmosphere of a temple. In this same area, a lighted fireplace under an atrium through which natural light penetrates gently invites the guests to take a seat as a ritual performance rather than a banal action.

In the remaining rooms, the same simple and exquisite architecture models spaces bathed in warm indirect lighting, rooms perfumed with oriental essences, beds that are an invitation to deep repose, a washbasin with an illuminated heart.

The visitor will be immediately struck by the openness and the simplicity of the materials and colours: beige Portland stone for the floors, black Belgian stone and granite in the bathrooms, golden chalk and sand colours for the lower floors, rust, grey or black for the upper floors.

All rooms have been individually designed to offer the discerning traveler an alternative, a modern definition of luxury: telephones, fax line, modem facility, air-conditioning, CD and video player, oxygen in the mini-bars.

There are four function rooms, private dining rooms, video conferencing facilities, libraries, fitness room, private apartments and even the temporary illusion of a tent in the Zen garden square or cocktails served on the terrace to 150 people.

For Anouska Hempel, the hotel's creator the Hempel is consequence of the desire for radical change. The result is a very special place that revolutionizes the concepts of travelling and accommodation in the threshold of a new century.

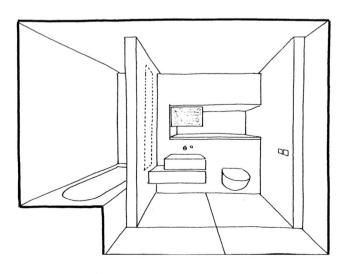

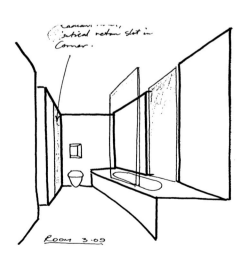

Room 3.09

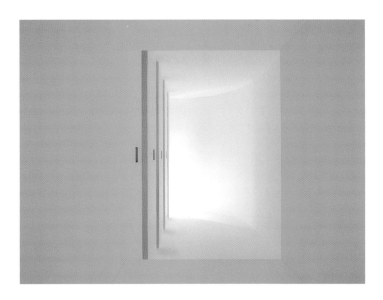

All the rooms have been designed independently. Nevertheless, in all of them a common interior design creates simple and exquisite spaces where light plays a leading role.

John Pawson

Walsh House

Telluride, California, USA

Photographs: Undine Pröhl

Central to the design of this house in the ski resort town of Telluride is its context of powerfully direct vernacular building forms. From the outside, the scale of the house is deceptively modest. With windows only on one of the side walls on the ground floor, the capacious interior volume of the second floor can hardly be guessed at. Once inside, the especially elongated single space of the upper floor is revealed and accentuated by placing the windows at both of the gable ends of the volume.

The public rooms (kitchen and living room) are on the upper floor, to take advantage of the mountain views through glazed gable ends, while bedrooms and bathrooms are on the ground floor.

By keeping to the east side of the building plot, the house maintains and enhances existing views. Likewise, each of the private rooms on the ground floor enjoys abundant natural light due to their being placed along the east wall; the long hallway and staircase are placed on the entirely closed west wall, where unwanted views of the neighboring constructions are completely blocked off.

The choice of exterior materials reflects the local palette, with quarry-cut stone flank walls, a weathered timber upper floor structure and a metal pitched roof. Inside, long straight lines and elongated forms create and heighten a sense of simplicity; the predominant materials here are stone or concrete for the floors, countertops and furnishings in wood and marble and sheets of frosted glass used as partitions.

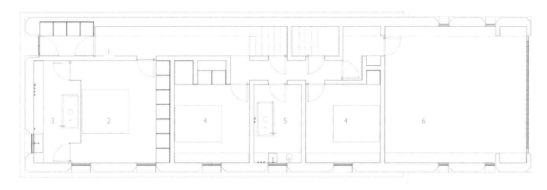

Ground floor plan

First floor plan

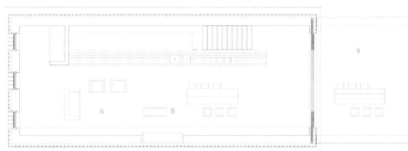

1. Entrance
2. Main bedroom
3. Main bathroom
4. Guest bedroom
5. Guest bathroom

6. Garage
7. Living area
8. Kitchen-dining
9. Terrace

Light-filled slits run the length of the room above the unusually long fireplace, where roof and wall intersect, as well as below it, where the marble bench meets the wall.

On the ground floor, the private rooms are pushed against the east wall to take advantage of the site's natural light. Sheets of frosted glass have been used as partitions between the bathrooms and bedrooms, thus further enhancing the lighting scheme. The flooring throughout the house is either stone or concrete, with bathroom and kitchen fixtures done predominantly in light-hued marble.

John Pawson

Maison Pawson

London, UK

Photographs: Richard Glover

This project was for the restoration of a dwelling in a Victorian terraced house in London. The façade of the building was left in its original state, except for the recession of the new entrance door leading to the raised ground floor where the two original reception rooms are transformed into one space. Here, both working fireplaces were retained.

A stone bench on the long wall acts as seating, hearth and light source. The interior atmosphere is minimal and comfortable. A table with benches and two chairs are the only furniture. On the opposite wall a row of pivoting doors conceals storage.

A new set of straight stairs lead to the bathroom. The bath, the floor, basin cube, and bench running around the edge of the room —which also contains the lavatory— are all made from the same cream colored stone. Gaps in the floor drain water from the shower mounted directly on the wall, and brimming over the edge of the bath. This is an attempt to capture some of the qualities with which bathing was once approached, more as a ritual than a hurried functional necessity.

On the same floor the two children's rooms have beds, shelves and desks in the same wood with corkboard forming one complete wall. The top floor, which is suffused with natural light, houses the main bedroom.

Materials are used as simply and directly as possible. The two white Carrara marble worktops, which are four inches thick and over fourteen feet long, are not mere surfaces, but elements in their own right. Holes have been cut into them for the marble sink and the iron cooking range.

With the exception of those that look onto the rear courtyard, the windows are made of etched glass. The kitchen was equipped with two large working areas made in Carrara marble.

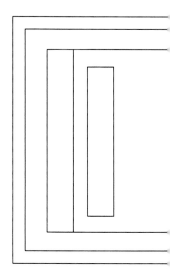

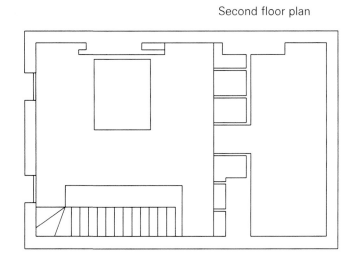

Second floor plan

First floor plan

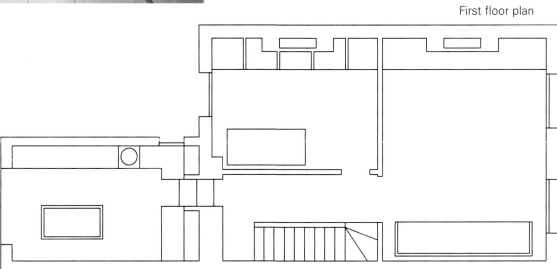

Ground floor plan

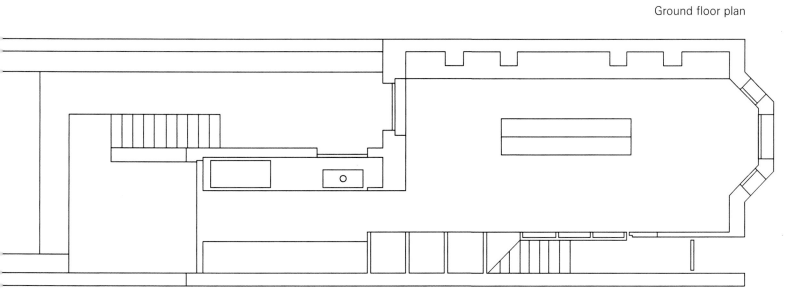

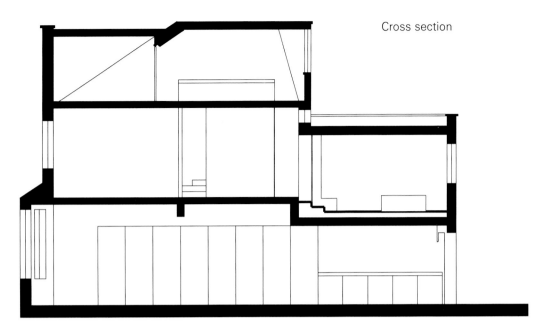

Cross section

In the bathroom, both the bathtub and the washbasin were made in stone of a soft cream colour. The floor and walls are clad in the same material.

John Pawson

Faggionato Apartment

London, UK

Photographs: Richard Glover

The apartment was to be created in part of a 1960s complex of laboratories built by the Gas Board in the heart of a south west suburb of London overlooking the river Thames. A developer had acquired the building when the Gas Board moved out and converted it into a series of shells for individual apartments. The clients had bought two of these units, which combined to form a vast L-shaped space of 600 sqm - the size of two or three conventional London terraced houses.

Here the clients were an art dealer and her financier husband. They had known the architect for some time. They realized that they were undertaking a whole new way of life —their previous home had been a very traditional apartment. The move required a new approach to domestic habits, new ways of dealing with possessions, indeed new possessions —the old furniture was not going to fit into so different an interior— and new ways for the couple of relating to each other and their children.

The architect wanted to create the sense of endless, unencumbered space. There was enough height to create a mezzanine level —in fact two mezzanine decks, one for parents, another for children and housekeeper— but also the scope to leave extensive areas of double-height space. As a result a sequence of spaces which incorporated both private and more open arrangements were provided.

The oak floors, laid in random widths, add rhythm and warmth to the interior spaces. The dining room and kitchen are accommodated under the mezzanine and screened from the main living area by a smoked glass wall. The three children´s bedrooms share a mezzanine deck. Two deep, stepped shelves form workspace overlooking the double height slice of space in front of the windows.

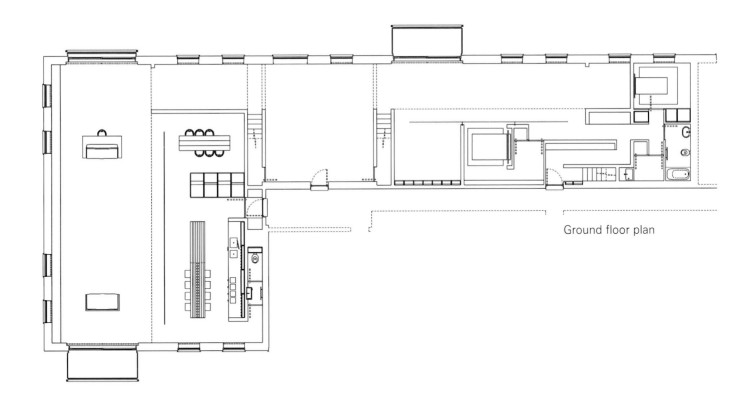

Ground floor plan

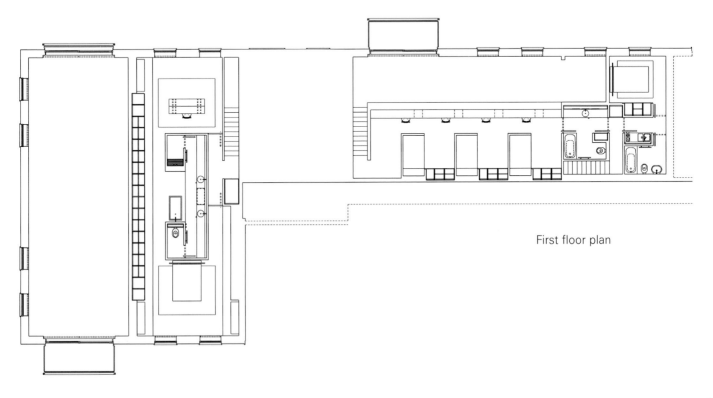

First floor plan

Bruce Kuwabara & Evan Webber

Residence and Studio in Richmond Hill

Ontario, Canada

Photograhs: Steven Evans

The design of the Reisman-Jenkinson Residence and Studio combines living and working spaces for a family of four in the suburban context of Richmond Hill, Ontario.

Four buildings constructed of light-grey, split faced concrete blocks are joined by three glazed linking elements to create a forecourt and garden courtyard.

Shaped roof elements on the sculpture studio and main living building are fabricated from anodized, formed aluminum panels. Fascias, coverings and cuppers complete each building and linking element.

The sculpture studio forms one edge of the forecourt. The interior receives indirect north light through clerestory windows.

A pair of doors constructed of Douglas fir open out onto the courtyard, framing views of a spectacular landscape of silver maple trees.

The conservatory entrance forms the opposite edge of the forecourt and connects the studio and main loft buildings. Simple volumes, high ceilings, large windows and door openings, and maple hardwood floors create the feel of a loft building. Fireplaces anchor the two ends of the living loft, while a pyramidal skylight establishes the kitchen space as a kind of third internal courtyard. Bedrooms and writing studios are grouped around the landscaped garden courtyard. Large sliding panels in the main loft and master bedroom buildings adjust the degree of privacy to create a flexible living arrangement.

In this work, architecture supports a vision of an alternative lifestyle in the suburbs. The design challenges conventional expectations about domesticity and celebrates the parallel existence of artistic practices and the rituals of daily life.

The maple-wood floor is an eye-catching feature of the interior, contrasting with the simple plastered walls..
The living-dining room area runs parallel to the street. The only notable furnishing element is the spacious kitchen located in a central position of the room.

Taku Sakaushi /O.F.D.A.

YAMA

Shibuya, Tokyo, Japan

Photographs: Hiroshi Ueda

As the site is raised a few meters in respect to the surroundings and the level of the road, privacy is automatically ensured on the ground floor of this light-filled and thoroughly modern home. Thus, at each corner of the site are placed large windows facing ample outdoor gardened spaces.

The second and third floors, on the other hand, are ensconced within pristine white volumes to shield them from views from the outside. An abundance of natural light is brought into these spaces through the incorporation of a vertical light shaft extending through three floors. The spatial dynamics brought about by this ground-floor horizontal openness paired with the sizeable vertical void create the central design theme, around which the house unfolds.

In fact the underlying and unavoidable question of shape and line when drawing up the floor plan was a central preoccupation in the design process of this house. This root question gave rise to the name: Yama, which means 'mountain' in Japanese. Rather than defining the shape of the house, it was meant as a symbolic anchoring concept.

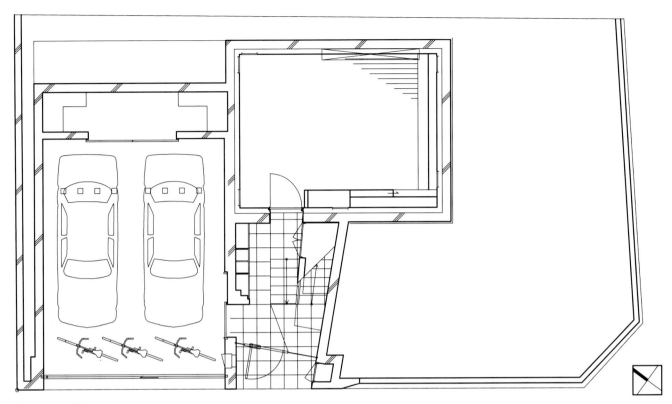

Basement Plan

Ground Floor Plan

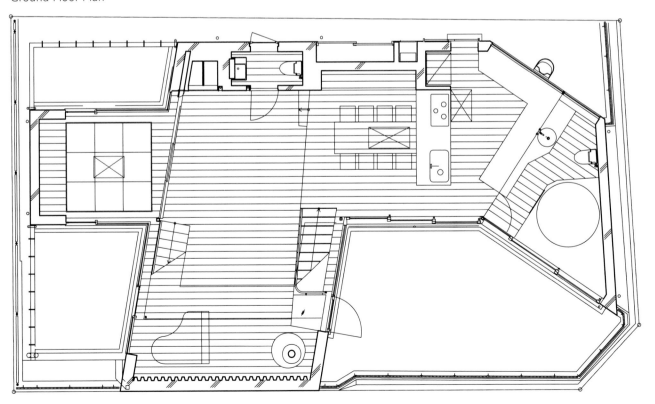

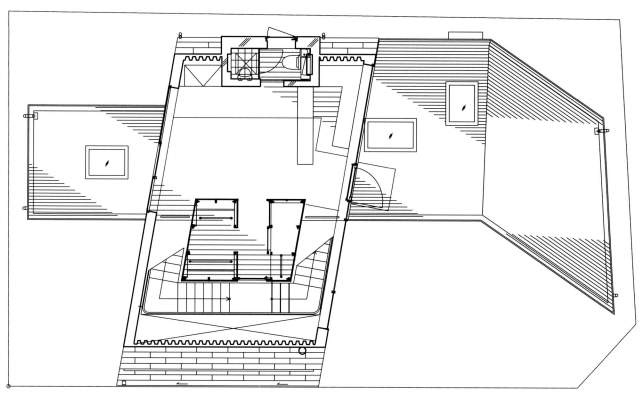

First Floor Plan

Second Floor Plan

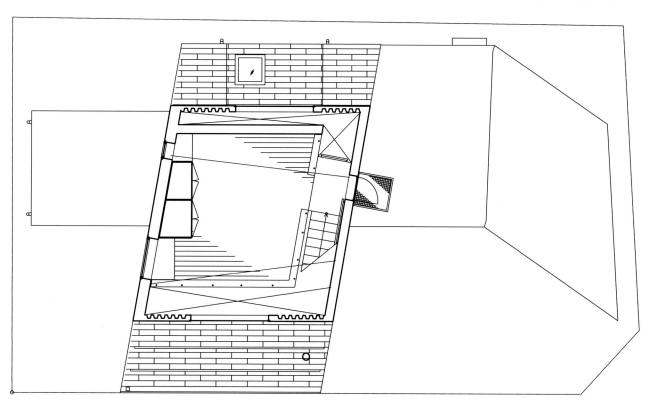

Graham Phillips

Skywood House

Middlessex, UK

Photographs: Nigel Young

The plot, etched into a densely populated zone, was subject to zoning laws which restricted the surface area available for construction to 250 sqm. The architect set out to create a "glass box" in the forest, a structure whose boundaries between interior and exterior would be blurred, where water would play a leading role.

The house, lying before the shores of a lake, is reached via a black gravel walkway which winds around the house, ending at the main patio at the back. The building rests on a grey limestone plinth, its bare, unadorned surface highlighting its simple shapes. Frameless glass doors covered by a pergola, a design echoed in the entrance to the garage, form the main entryway. A noteworthy element in the exterior space is the main chimney, which hides the drainage system, the pipes and the ventilation system within a single unit. The dwelling is unified by long, 3-meter-high walls which reach beyond the enclosed spaces toward the lake and surrounding terrain, thereby defining footpaths. This minimalist expression contrasts with the wealth of the landscape, creating a serene and wondrous experience.

The dwelling is enclosed by two glass wings, the first of which, at a height of 3 meters, forms the volume containing the four bedrooms and their respective bathrooms. This module comprises one of the sides of a completely enclosed garden, which has a square lawn lying over a border of black gravel.

The glass volume which houses the sitting room is the tallest, thereby highlighting the steel sheet which comprises the floating roof. The main space enjoys breathtaking views across the lake to the west, toward the island, becoming as much a focal point by night as by day.

The tiling of the sitting room continues outward toward the garden, through a glass facade, blurring the boundaries between interior and exterior. This space is organized like a double square: the sitting room is defined by a 3.6 sqm carpet centered over limestone flooring, a motif —that of a square framed within another background— which is seen again in the inside patio and the garden at the back. In the kitchen/dining room, a combination of sliding panels and two moveable tables allow a distribution which can be altered according to its users' needs.

Limestone and glass, used both inside and out, confer homogeneity on the building and continuity between the exterior and interior. The entirety of the water, electrical and ventilation systems are operated through a single vertical duct, while the heating system is under the floor, thereby avoiding the need for radiators. The furniture and other decorative elements have been custom-designed for this home.

East-west section through lake, living-room and courtyard

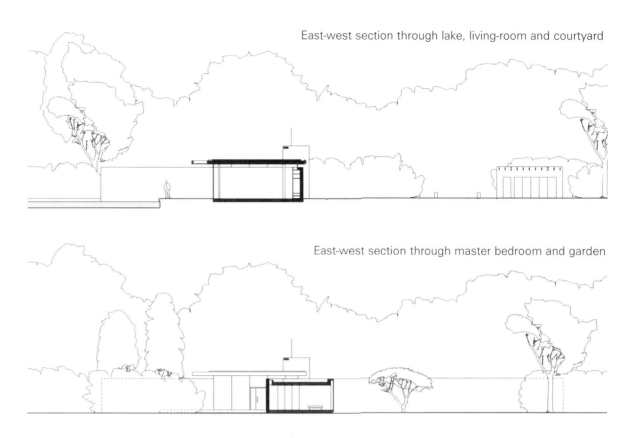

East-west section through master bedroom and garden

Ground floor plan

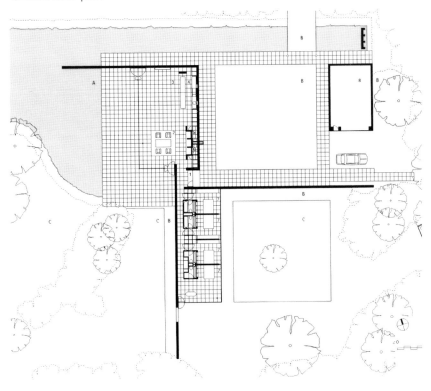

Koen van Velsen

Vos Family House

Amsterdam, The Netherlands

Photographs: Duccio Malagamba

The Vos House, designed by the firm of Koen van Velsen, is located on the Island of Borneo in the port of Amsterdam, opposite a canal. It is a narrow terraced house whose impressive facade distinguishes it from the surrounding buildings. The facade has been solved as a screen that allows an "urban garden" to be created in the part of the dwelling that opens onto the street. This is an imaginative and innovative approach, since it breaks with the traditional idea of the back garden; each floor has an interior terrace that opens onto the street.

The scheme is distributed on three floors. The ground floor houses the garage, from which the dwelling is accessed by means of a staircase. Glass walls separate the interior of the house from the terrace that gives onto the street behind the screen, whose glazed windows let natural light into the interior. A large tree stands in the inner courtyard, rising through the different floors of the dwelling in its vertical progression.

The organization of the dwelling spaces is another example of the architect's audacity. The most spectacular feature is the design of the kitchen and dining room. A wall separates these two spaces and acts as a storage space on the kitchen side.

The particularity of this wall is that it is mobile and allows the kitchen to be made larger or smaller according to the needs. Versatility was one of the requirements of the client, who wanted a flexible dwelling that could adapt to changes.

Chromatic uniformity is a feature of the whole dwelling, with flat polished surfaces. The spaces are separated by walls that act as storage spaces and maintain order in the dwelling. The space is bright and sober, flooded with natural light through all the windows and through the skylights located on the top floor.

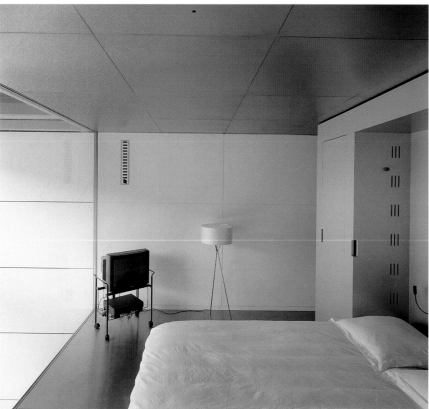

Basement plan

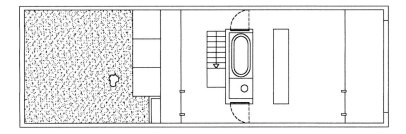

Ground floor plan

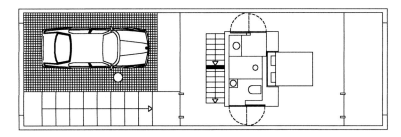

First floor plan

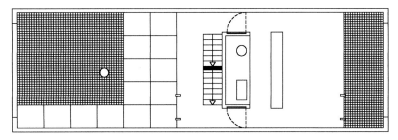

Second floor plan

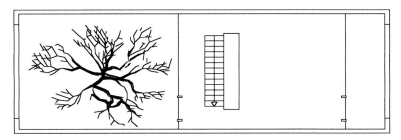

Roof floor plan

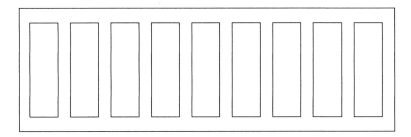

Eugeen Liebaut

Verhaeghe House

Sint Pieters Leeuw, Belgium

Photographs: Saskia Vanderstichele

The program for this house near Brussels was chosen from among ten competing architectural studios. The Verhaeghe house is a simple two-story structure with a flat roof, hemmed in on both sides by neighboring buildings. Since the site itself was seven meters wide and zoning restrictions would only allow a height of six meters, a modest volume had to be designed.

With such spatial restrictions, the architects decided to make room by sinking the ground floor 80cm to the level of the foundation masonry. Financially, this is a simple enough operation; while the advantages gained in spatial configuration are highly attractive.

The living room is a high-ceilinged, transparent space. Here, the inhabitants move freely about between two strategically-placed volumes - the kitchen and the toilet - which do not reach the full height of the ceiling. Together, these volumes form a screen of sorts within the transparent volume which provides the necessary privacy from the public street. The high and wide glass facade rises from an incision between the volume and the socle like a rare and floating object.

The rear facade is also entirely glazed, making the steel-grated terrace outside seem like a continuation of the dwelling. By working with grates, the bedrooms on the ground floor are ensured sufficient light. This relatively small house enjoys a spatiality which many a majestic villa can only dream of.

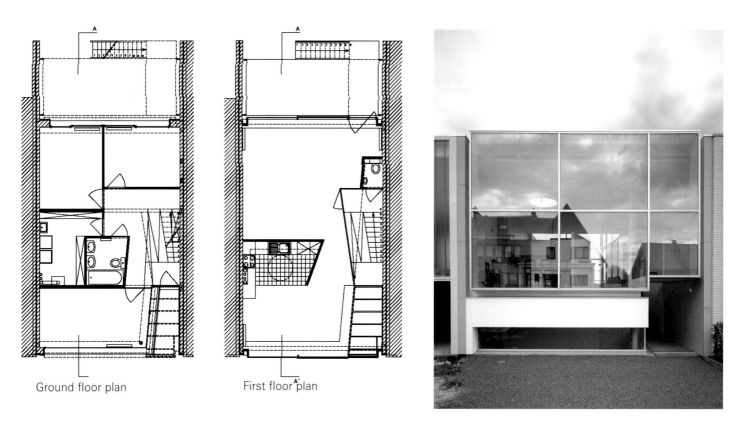

Ground floor plan   First floor plan

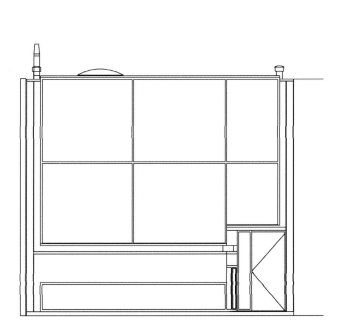

Front elevation

Site plan

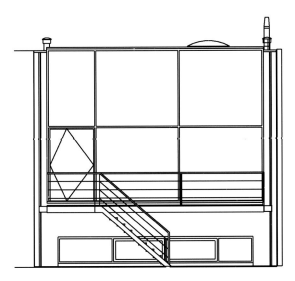

Back elevation

Norisada Maeda

Borzoi House

Katsuura Chiba, Japan

Photographs: Hiroshi Shinozawa

The highly experimental design for this house arose from two very specific requirements from the client. On one hand, she stipulated that the home should provide a sense of security, a feeling of looking inward; and on the other, she wanted to ensure that her pet dog, a borzoi, could not get out easily. Added to this was the architect's own passion for surfing, which he translated into the very layout in the form of a breaking wave.

"All is one inside a curving wave. Just as all the air for the living space within this giant metal curve is one," says Maeda. Thus, the floor plan for this single-story home is simple, punctuated only by three voids which bring ample light into the home and which have been filled with abundant vegetation, thereby avoiding a sense of confinement.

So, while Borzoi is "one air", there are paradoxes arrayed therein so that multiple sceneries unfurl simultaneously. The three gardens provide the necessary counterpoint to the spatial continuum of floor, walls and ceiling all being formed by the same curving surface. While the external view is a unified whole, the internal space displays obvious contours.

The structure is timber frame and steel, with the exterior completely sheathed in metal. Upon entering, though, the hard industrial feel instantly becomes gentle and welcoming, with the interior clad almost entirely in white gypsum plaster board.

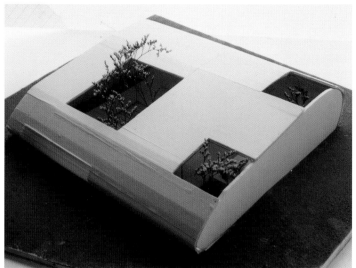

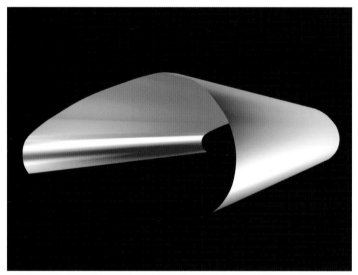

The structure is timber frame and steel, with the exterior completely sheathed in metal. Upon entering, though, the hard industrial feel instantly becomes gentle and welcoming, with the interior clad almost entirely in white gypsum plaster board.

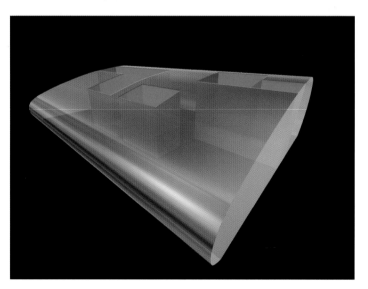

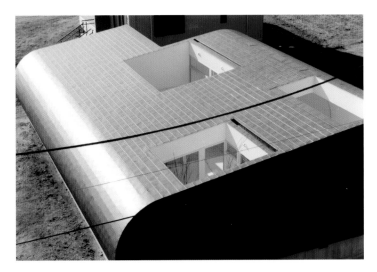
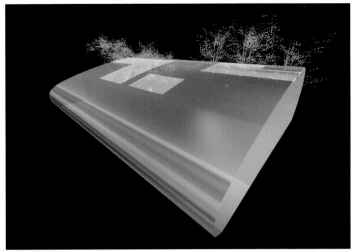

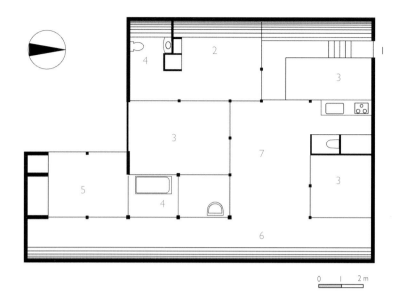

1. Entry
2. Bedroom
3. Garden
4. Bathroom
5. Tatami room
6. Dog run
7. Lounge

0   1   2 m

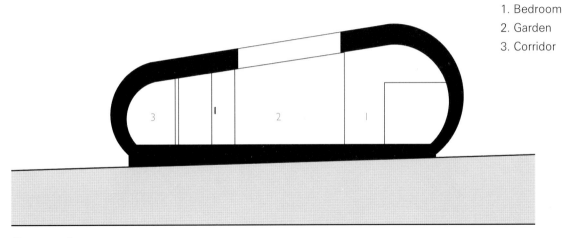

1. Bedroom
2. Garden
3. Corridor

Cross section

0   1   2 m

Akira Sakamoto

Hakuei Residence

Mino, Osaka, Japan

Photographs: Yoshiharu Matsumura

The site is sandwiched between streets to the east and west. Moreover, the site is at the head of a T-intersection on the west side. These conditions generate an east-west flow on the site.

The building, made up of one wall and the three rectangular parallelepipeds, has no core. The whole space is made by four elements, a white wall and three white boxes. The basic concept was to see how to draw the inside to outside and to create a flow of space by means of these presences.

First, a wall was erected on the south side, following the east-west direction of flow, and a 17 meter deep space on an east-west axis was created. That space was divided into a west building, a courtyard and an east building, and a 3 x 4.5 meter rectangular parallelepiped with a deck was arranged on top of the east building. The axial spaces of these three rectangular parallelepipeds overlap and face each other, resulting in an integrated whole. Moreover they take the flow of the street to the west and guide it east and lead the eyes of passers by from west to east.

The space is articulated simply and sectioned by discontinous walls, with openings in the walls creating continuity. Space flows continously, through the window in the atelier, the courtyard, the bathroom and the small garden outside the bathroom. People look or talk across the courtyard and the deck.

Physical movement and the consciousness of things happening beyond walls create links. The sharp light introduced by the toplight, the soft light spreading across surfaces, and the movement of light reflected on white walls communicate a sense of nature and a feeling of the passing of time which are transmitted throughout the entire building.

This building does not require room names. Visitors are not greeted by a vestibule but by the building as a whole. The residents look skyward between rooms, are made aware of the sunlight and the wind, and pass the time in each place within the house conscious of change. "During the daytime, the white walls reflecting the sun light becomes soft, at the same time, the light make a sharp line from a skylight on the wall. At night, the wall shows new rhythms on its surface and the light spreads over the wall and the room. We can feel at home by all these elements making the residence" (A. Sakamoto).

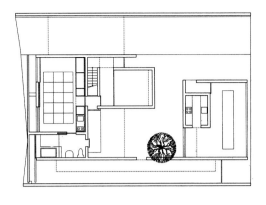

Ground floor plan

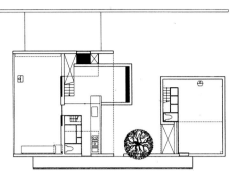

First floor plan

The architect used great care in dealing with the entry of light into the rooms of the dwelling.

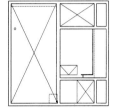
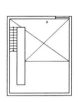

Second floor plan

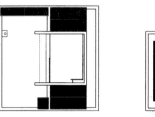

Roof plan

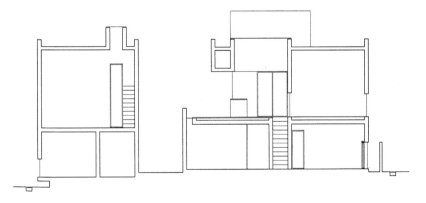

Longitudinal sections

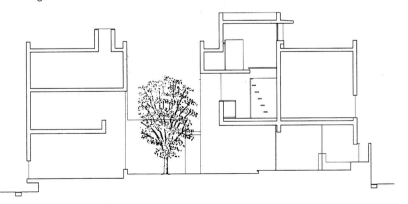

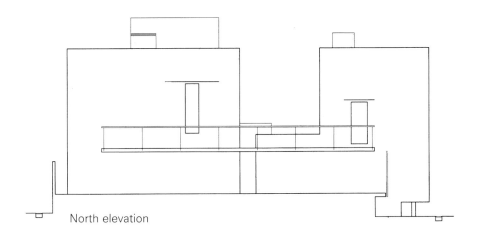

North elevation

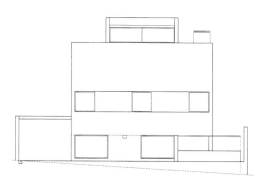

East elevation (east building)

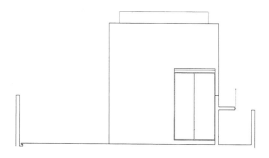

East elevation (west building)

Hiroyuki Arima
House in Dazaifu

Dazaifu, Japan

Photographs: Koji Okamoto

This house is a device to provide natural views, and to include light into scenes of life positively. Here the value of space focuses on how to give man nature rather than functionality and efficiency as a place to live a life. That is, it is composed by the combination of some spaces resulting from the consideration of views, light and wind, and life thus follows the order of spaces determined in relation to the exterior. This residence therefore has a standard of value which is apparently different from the ordinary Japanese residence of to-day, and is much closer to the classical one.

The residence is located not too far from the approach to Dazaifu Shrine. The surroundings are silent and do not give the impression that one is close to a tourist spot. The ground here is uneven, and native bamboo groves and broadleaf trees provide pleasing views with the changing seasons. Two boxes are placed on the slope at a difference in level of 10 meters, facing the hills of Dazaifu. Each one is completely independent at its elevation.

The role of the lower box is to cut off the distant views horizontally and to expose the various changes of nature to the interior. Here, the views play an essential part in composing spaces as an element. The interior spaces have no concept of a room. The "box" forms a large room by itself. In it, the small boxes with functional elements, which form the unit arranging the function of life efficiently, are placed with order. The upper volume also reveals functional elements of the interior.

The upper box opens only vertically, and its role is to separate the interior from the exterior. It consists of two spaces, a light garden with a shallow pool of water, and beyond that Gallery 2. In this space, the resident can select various light shows by changing operable partitions. If necessary, the interior can be completely separated from the exterior. The visual relationship between man and nature in the upper volume is thus purer than in the lower volume.

The two boxes are connected by a natural path along the inclination of the slope. To live by coming and going between the two volumes means that a part of nature is naturally inserted into the living space.

155

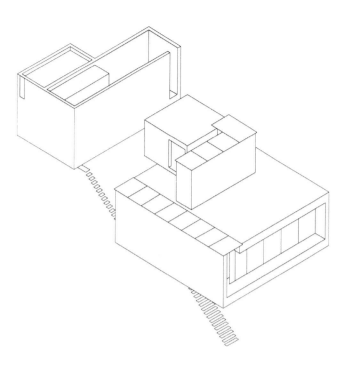

The dwelling consists of a single space inside which small containers house the most functional elements.

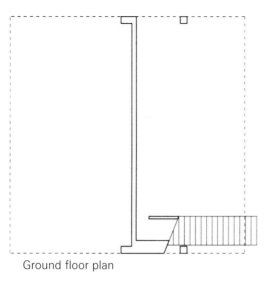

Ground floor plan

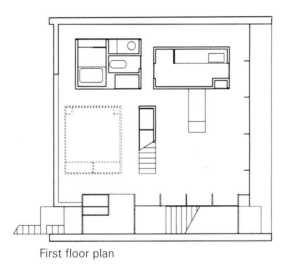

First floor plan

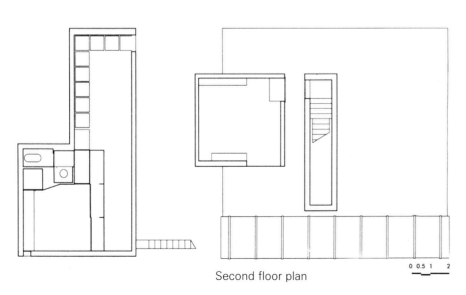

Second floor plan

0 0.5 1   2

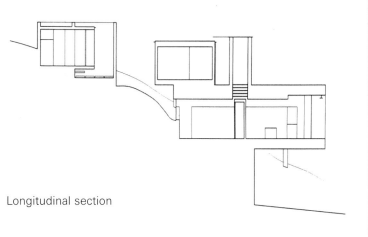

Longitudinal section

159

Hiroyuki Arima

House 3R

Fukuoka, Japan

Photographs: Koji Okamoto

The building is located some distance from the city center on a site studded with different kinds of trees such as maple and cherry, whose aspect varies with the seasons.

The scheme is a conversion of a small old apartment house to provide a favorable environment for living. Although there was nothing particularly unique about the 20-year-old building, a residential law banned any alterations to the outer appearance. The structures are on a northern slope with the front road on the third floor level, and access to the maisonette is possible only by going underground by stairs at road level.

"3r" (3 reeds) means three units of a movable wooden wall panel which is deployed near the entrance of the maisonette. Since the three units revolve independently of each other, it is possible for a resident to select diverse spatial variations. There are no specific restrictions governing the spatial configuration.

The former interior furnishings in the space have all been demolished and the floors, walls and ceilings are all painted white to make the most of the weak sunlight on the north side. The entire space constitutes a huge continuous structure.

Several necessary functions, such as the installation area, bedroom and sanitary rooms, are deployed continuously along two floors while being connected by a stairwell. The outer walls with the existing sash windows are all covered with translucent plastic panels from the inside. Holes in a variety of diameters have been punched into the surface of the wooden and plastic panels.

The surfaces that enclose the apartment's floors, walls and roof were painted white in order to reflect and multiply the scarce light from the north that penetrates through the existing openings. These were clad in translucent plastic panels.

Though it is organized on two different floors, the apartment constitutes a single continuous space, thereby offering a wide variety of visual perspectives.

A steep slender stairway with a metal skeleton and wooden steps communicates the floor that gives access to the dwelling with the lower level on which most of the private rooms are located.

The wide range of positions of the three mobile wooden panels provide the owner with numerous options for configuring the space.

Engelen Moore
House in Redfern

Sydney, Australia

Photographs: Ross Honeysett

This two-story house has been built on a vacant plot of land formerly occupied by two terrace houses, in a street otherwise composed of houses, warehouses and apartments of varying ages and sizes. The local council insisted that it read as two terrace-type houses rather than as a warehouse. The front elevation is divided into two vertical bays. The major horizontal elements are aligned with the adjoining terraced houses, and each bay relates to these houses proportionally. The internal planning reflects this two-bay arrangement at the front, while the rear elevation expresses the full 6m high, 7m wide internal volume. There was a very limited budget for this project, so a simple strategy was developed to construct a low-cost shell composed of a steel portal framed structure with concrete block external skins on the long sides, lined internally with plasterboard. The front and rear parapets and blade walls are clad with compressed fiber cement sheets. This shell is painted white throughout. Within this white shell are placed a series of more refined and rigorously detailed elements differentiated by their aluminum or grey paint finish.

The front elevation is made up of six vertical panels, the lower level being clad in Alucobond aluminum composite sheet, the left hand panel being the 3.3m high front door, and the three panels on the right hand side forming the garage door. The upper level is made up of operable extruded aluminum louvers, enabling it to be adjusted from transparency to opacity.

The 6m high west-facing glass wall is made up of six individual panels, which slide and stack to one side, allowing the entire rear elevation to be opened up. This not only spatially extends the interior into the courtyard, but also, in combination with the louvered front elevation, allows exceptional control of cross ventilation to cool the house in summer, while allowing very good solar penetration to warm the house in winter. In summer, this western glass wall is screened from the sun by a large eucalyptus tree on the adjoining property.

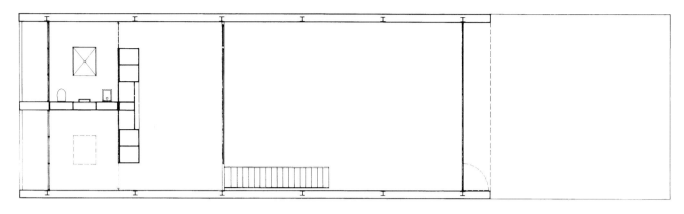

First floor plan

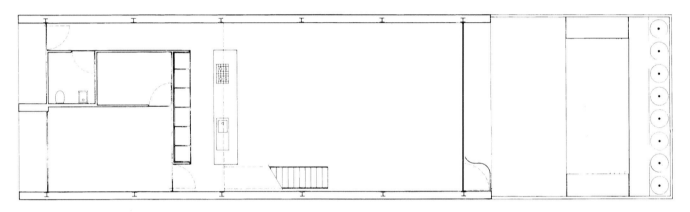

Ground floor plan

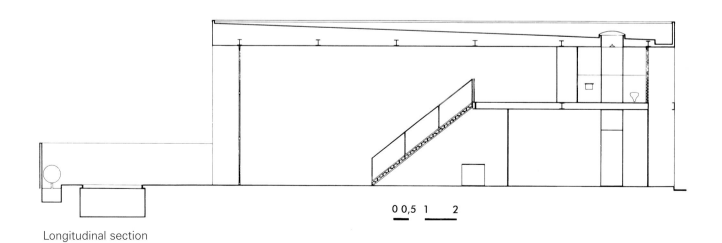

0 0,5 1   2

Longitudinal section

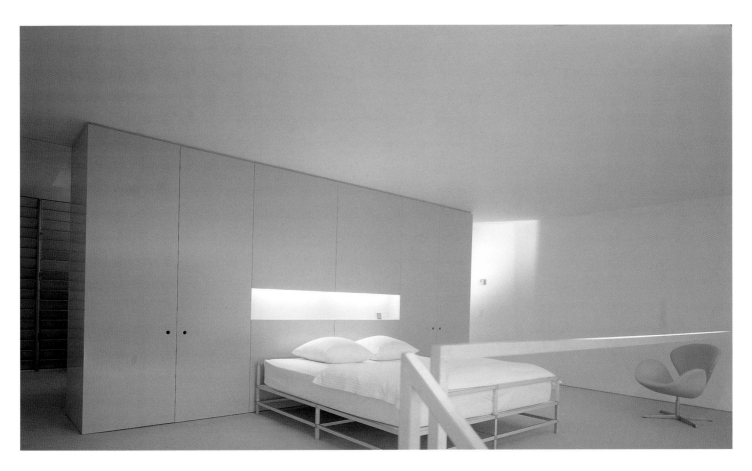

The rooms of the upper floor are fitted with mobile aluminum shutters that can be adjusted to allow for complete transparency or opacity.

The furniture was designed by the architects. The basic requirements were that they should be inexpensive and lightweight for easy mobility.

Dean / Wolf Architect

Urban Interface Loft

New York City, USA

Photographs: Peter Aaron / Esto

The Urban Interface Loft can be seen as an idea about dwelling below a ground plane, etc. the recreated urban ground plane. This new horizon/ground line is formed by the consistent five-six store y roof line of the buildings surrounding Duane Park. The roof plane is sliced open to the sky, revealing the landscape of both the sky and its relation to the city. At the same time, the new urban ground plane drops into the centre of the loft. Creating both visual and physical passage, the contrast between below and above is heightened through this connection.

The lower realm attains a new centre. Its deep interior creates an exterior realm removed from the urban landscape. This slicing of the original shell of the building allows for the insertion of the domestic realm of the loft. Lined in copper, it slides from interior to exterior linking these two public realms of the loft.

Displaced and idealised, this new centre becomes a haunting space of slow passage. The movement into and out of the apartment inhabits a space of continual fluctuation. Both exterior and interior as well as hot and cold. This voided centre which is never at rest begins an interior landscape with a multiplicity of views from its inhabited perimeter. Opened and closed to vision as well as to physical passage, the coding of transparency and translucency conceals and reveals the degree of privacy of its adjacent program. The bedrooms are shielded from gaze through the lower zone of translucency. Across the void, sight from the living spaces slips easily between inside and out.

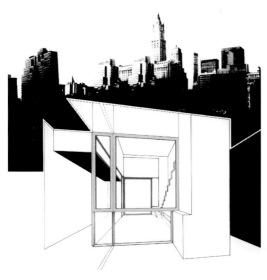 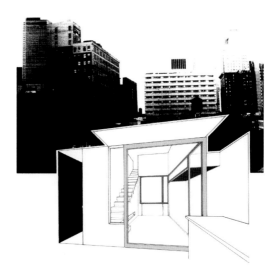

Axonometric view

Axonometrc view

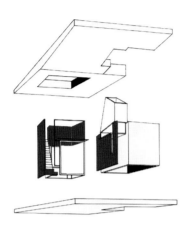

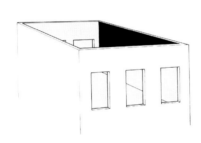

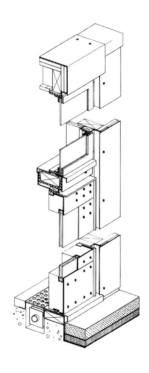

Construction detail
of the window

Sugiura Office

House H

Nagoya, Japan

Photographs: Tamoutsu Kurumada

House H is located in a narrow site surrounded by neighboring buildings. In Japan, this configuration is known as "Unagi no Nedoko" or "the nest of an eel", and it is common in traditional city-house districts in Kyoto, presenting special privacy and space problems for new buildings. This particular site is open to the north, where there is a busy road. The clients wanted to avoid having windows looking out to the road, but they still hoped to have a bright and open house.

Within this narrow site, the architects placed the volume leaving a 2.5 m strip of land to the south and a 1 m strip to the east. These spaces are used to help guide the light and air to the interior in order to create an open feeling inside.

The largest openings were placed on the south side to allow as much direct sunlight as possible into the building. Frosted glass for diffused light was placed on the east-facing side of the first floor. On the western side where there is no setback at all from the neighbors, skylights were designed to allow the light to filter through the roof and floor down to the first floor. At the northern end of the second floor, a kind of chimney acts as a vent to allow air to flow from the south to the north. The resulting space manages to have free flowing air and three different types of light - direct, diffused and changing light - to create a house that feels open.

The structure was designed to take up minimum space. Although it is actually a hybrid that uses both frames and Vierendeel structures, to the observer it appears like a simple box.

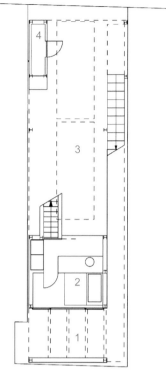

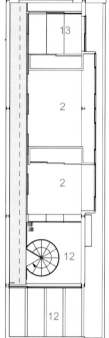

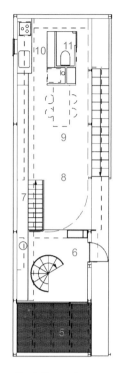

4

10 | 11

13

3

9

2

8

7

2

6

2

1

5

12

12

Ground floor plan

First floor plan

Second floor plan

1. Court
2. Bedroom
3. Parking
4. Storage
5. Terrace
6. Entrance
7. Counter
8. Living
9. Dining
10. Kitchen
11. Lavatory
12. Void
13. Tatami room

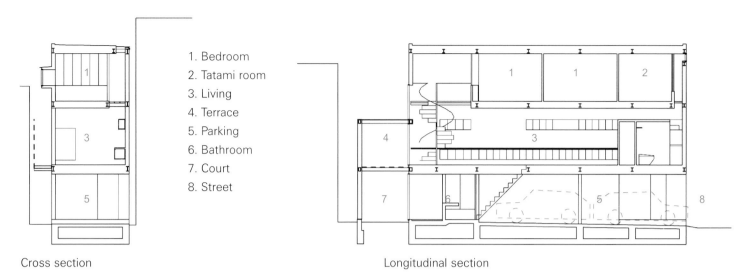

1. Bedroom
2. Tatami room
3. Living
4. Terrace
5. Parking
6. Bathroom
7. Court
8. Street

Cross section   Longitudinal section

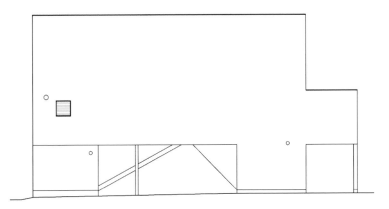

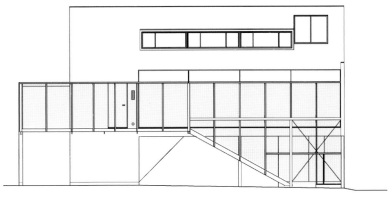

West elevation

East elevation

The architects use three types of light - direct, diffused and changing light - to bring as much light as possible into the interior while maintaining privacy from the surrounding buildings.

Takao Shiotsuka

Atu House

Ohnojo-city, Fukuoka Prefecture, Japan

Photographs: Kaori Ichikawa

The site is on the boundary where the residential area meets the forest. The tiered landscape and a small waterway are the main geographical features, and it is surrounded by trees. A little sunlight penetrates through the foliage, creating the appealing feeling of a dense forest. The architects decided to bring the external environment into the interior of the house through the design and the choice of construction materials.

In three directions, the building is used as a large glass window, with the color of the surrounding trees projected onto its surface. The weather outside and the passing of time changes the expression of the house at each moment. A glass window reaches from the floor to a height of about 1.8 meters, and minimizes the need for artificial light. The glazed patterned glass abstracts the scenery to a green-hued mosaic. In order to bring the surrounding green deep into the interior of the rooms, the indoor furniture and other materials are white.

The architects and the client preferred to secure a bigger space rather than highly finished materials. The high-ceilinged space effectively enhances the surroundings in the shape of a tiered stand for dolls, with a height difference indoors. A middle floor is used to project the ventilation and colors of the trees indoors.

The circular light from the ceiling changes according to the different sized spaces, giving the appearance of a random effect and mirroring the environment that is constantly changing. The outer wall is a wave-like steel plate, which reflects the color of the sky and the trees.

"ATU" is the name of the daughter of the house. Her physical disability, which means she can't go into the outdoors by herself, inspired the concept of the house. The idea, which was successfully realized, was to project the surrounding scenery inside and envelop the space and the family in the green forest.

The design and construction materials draw the spacious feeling and natural colors of the surrounding landscape into the interior of the house. The large glazed windows that dominate the house minimize the need for artificial light and create a constantly changing patterns based on the weather conditions outside.

Jo Crepain Architect NV

Feyen Residence

Sint-Pieters-Leeuw, Belgium

Photographs: Ludo Noël

This private residence for a family of four is located on the Wilderveld housing development in Sint-pieters-leeuw on the outskirts of the municipality. It is not, in itself, a particularly spectacular planning area, with building plots measuring only seven meters in width set aside for terraced housing and others that are ten meters wide for semi-detached housing. What is special about this project, however, is the fact that the prospective homeowners have the opportunity to choose from a limited number of architects so as to ensure the quality of the design.

The final program for this house was a simple beam-shaped volume with a slightly lowered sleeping area in order to ensure maximum headroom for the living area within the prescribed maximum building height of six meters. The dimensions of the living area are 7x12.50 m and 3.30 m in height, interrupted only by a cube-shaped volume housing the kitchen and the home office.

This volume is finished on all sides with opalescent polycarbonate sheets illuminated by fluorescent lights, creating at night the impression of a glowing ice cube.

The spacious entrance hall leads to an intermediate landing with a gently-sloping ramp falling off to the left towards the three bedrooms, bathroom, toilet and storage space. Just opposite the entryway is a 1.5-meter-wide staircase leading to the living area situated 2.2 meters above ground level. All of the flooring is made from mechanically finished concrete, beneath which has been installed gas-fired under-floor heating throughout the house; the stairs and ramps have been clad in galvanized sheet metal.

A terrace measuring 14 sqm is connected to the garden via stairs that are approximately two meters wide. The use of basic materials coupled with a straightforward design concept has effectively allowed for strict adherence to the allotted budget.

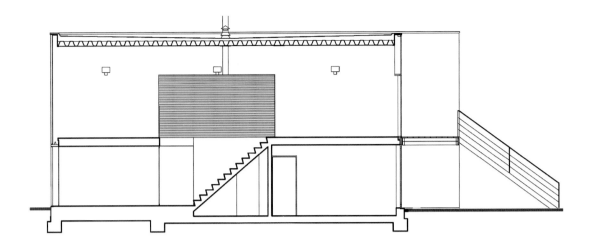

Longitudinal sections

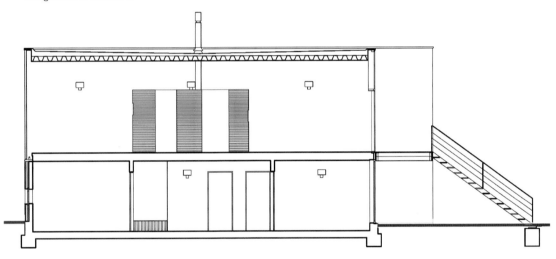

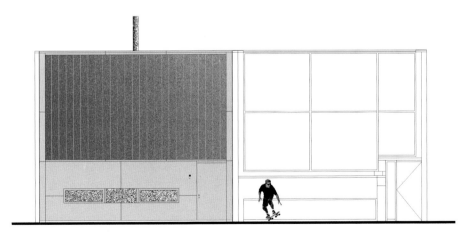

North elevation

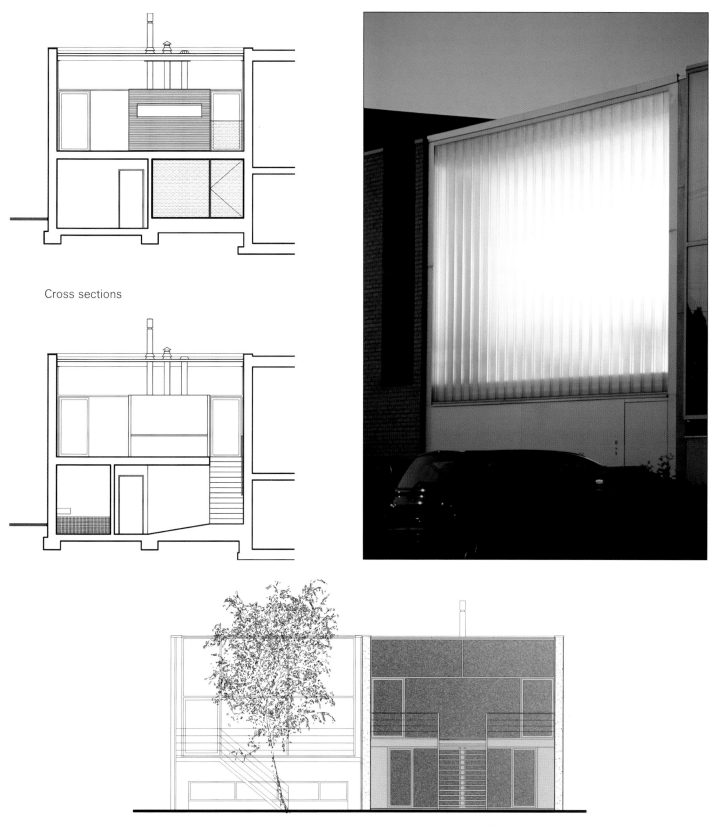

Cross sections

South elevation

The dimensions of the living area are 7x12.50 m, and 3.30 m in height, interrupted only by a cube-shaped volume housing the kitchen and the home office.

This volume is finished on all sides with opalescent polycarbonate sheets illuminated by fluorescent lights, creating at night the impression of a glowing ice cube.

Chiba Manabu Architects
Kashima Surf Villa

Kashima, Japan

Photographs: Nácàsa & Partners

Located just meters from a long stretch of sandy beach, effectively separating land and water, Kashima Surf Villa possesses an architecture of dialect between private and public spaces and functions, all in harmony with the existing "natural" tension between the ocean and the beach.

Conceived as a shared, corporate villa for a group of friends, where both intimacy and communal gathering imposed their own sets of requirements, the architect succeeded in creating two pairs of connected, yet separate, spatial entities.

On one hand, two box-like shapes define the private space of the 9 bedrooms, grouping 5 north-facing rooms on the first floor, and another 4 south-facing rooms in the upper box. In each box, the color of the interior walls counterbalances the effect of natural light: with white in the rooms facing the north and black in those facing the south, a light equilibrium is consequently created.

On the other hand, the consequence of creating these two "diagonally positioned" boxes is that the "negative space" creates another diagonal direction, visually tying a pair of shared/public spaces, the 1st floor to the 2nd floor.

Remarkably, standard notions of 1st and 2nd floor divisions disappear here, giving a new dimension to the perception of levels inside the house: the 2nd floor is immediately felt here as being the roof of the first box. From the first floor, one climbs a stairway leading to this "inner roof", accentuated by the use of the wooden parquet as flooring. To highlight more this roof/floor effect, the 2nd box of bedrooms is positioned higher than the 2nd floor, standing independently from the rest of the space, and creating a third floor.

It is because of this leveling method that an exciting small space was created, sandwiched in between these two surfaces: behind the top of the stairway, a low-height space forces the dweller to sit on the floor, as in a tea room, contemplating the ocean in the horizon.

Although this dialect of two intertwining spaces has appeared in some of the architect's previous residential designs, the spatial gap in Kashima Surf Villa between the two poles is obviously wider.

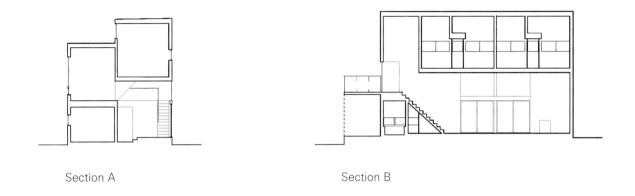

Section A

Section B

Chiba Manabu Architects

House in Black

Tokyo, Japan

Photographs: Nacása & Partners

This is a small house for a young couple on the outskirts of Tokyo, standing on a corner of a block at the end of a downhill road close to the Tama River. It is a simple cubic volume which involves three floor plates set on the center of the site.

The first floor has been scooped out as if to make a crossing integrated with the T-junction in front of the house. On the second floor, the skin has been peeled off to create windows and to bring the surrounding landscape into a more intimate relationship with the house.

There is also a slit cut out as a terrace on the third floor to mediate the two environmental elements that determine the character of this area; the hill and the river. Additionally, there are well holes at the four corners on the third floor, thereby making this level a bit smaller than the other two. Along with the staircase going through the center, a void connects the three floors gently and ambiguously.

The whole architecture composed in this way has an unstable outline and a permeable interior space. The architecture aims to create a new urban landscape that results from making a mutual relationship between the surrounding environment and itself. Furthermore, the idea was to merge the relationship between urban space and architecture, ensuring enclosed spaces for privacy while also creating a sense of transparency and views toward the public surroundings. This feeling of being both here and there, inside and out is one of the most essential charms of living in the city.

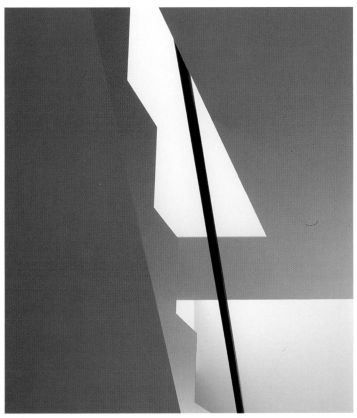

Ground floor plan
1. Entrance
2. Porch
3. Corridor
4. Piano room
5. Studio
6. Toilet

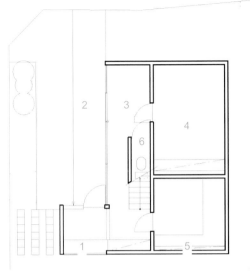

First floor plan
1. Living / Dining room
2. Kitchen
3. Child's room
4. Japanese style room

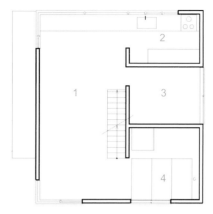

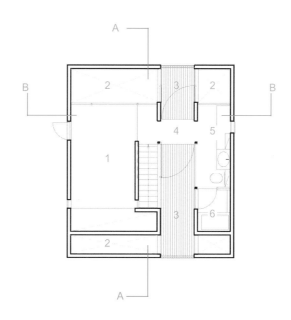

Second floor plan
1. Bed room
2. Void
3. Terrace
4. Corridor
5. Lavatory
6. Bathroom

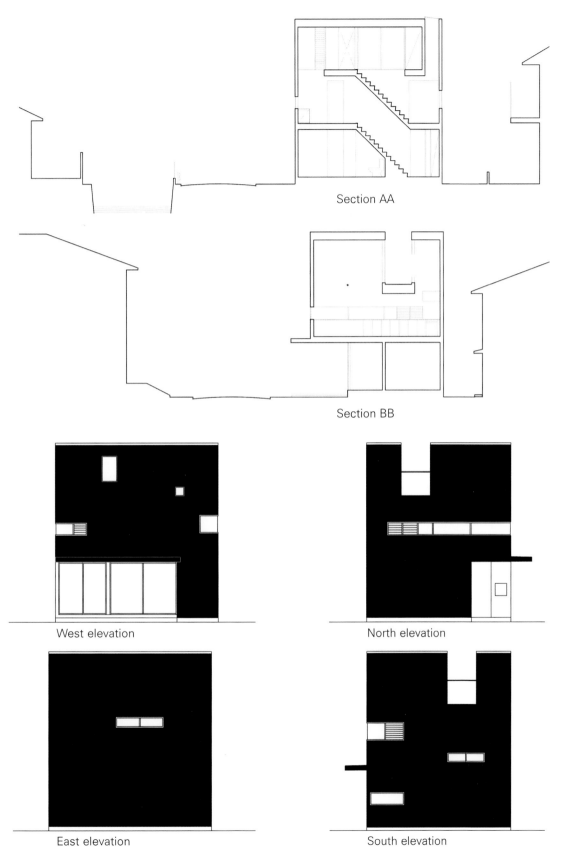

Section AA

The house is based on a simple cubic volume that has been treated architecturally in order to respond to its environment. The metaphors of scooping out parts of the volume or peeling away the skin were applied to the basic shape in order to create an equilibrium between interior and exterior, house and surroundings.

Section BB

West elevation

North elevation

East elevation

South elevation

235